This book was compiled by
with the A.I assistance o

## **Dedication**

I hope this helps all of my wonderful
readers achieve all their goals in their
business. And I would like to thank my
wonderful wife for all of her continued
support in all my ventures.

©Daniel Melehi

May 7 2023

# Contents

# Chapter 1: Understanding the Changing Landscape of Work

As we move deeper into the 21st century, the nature of work is changing at an unprecedented pace. In this chapter, we will take a closer look at the forces driving this change.

## SUBCHAPTER 1.1: THE HISTORY OF WORK

Work has always been a fundamental part of human society, from hunting and gathering to factory work and beyond. Throughout history, work has been shaped by culture, technology, and economic systems.

Understanding how work has evolved over time is key to understanding the changes we are currently experiencing.

## SUBCHAPTER 1.2: TECHNOLOGICAL ADVANCEMENTS

One of the greatest drivers of change in the modern workforce is technology. From the mechanization of agriculture to the development of the internet, technology has always played a central role in shaping how we work. Today, advancements in robotics, artificial intelligence, and machine learning are transforming entire industries.

## SUBCHAPTER 1.3: AUTOMATION AND ARTIFICIAL INTELLIGENCE

Automation and artificial intelligence are among the most significant disruptors in the modern workplace. These technologies are changing the way we think about work, often rendering certain jobs obsolete while creating new opportunities in others. In this subchapter, we will explore how these technologies are changing the very nature of work itself.

# THE HISTORY OF WORK

Work has been a central part of human life for thousands of years. Throughout history, humans have engaged in various forms of work, from hunting and gathering to agriculture and manufacturing. In ancient societies, work was often tied to religious or communal practices, with individuals contributing to the community in exchange for protection and sustenance. As societies became more complex, work became more specialized, with individuals focusing on specific tasks or trades. This led to the rise of guilds and other organizations that regulated work and provided training and support for workers. During the Industrial Revolution, work underwent a major transformation as manual labor was replaced by machinery and automation. This led to the rise of factories and the development of new industries, creating new jobs and economic opportunities. In the 20th century, work continued to evolve as technology advanced and new industries emerged. The rise of the knowledge economy saw the growth of industries such as finance, healthcare, and technology, while service-based industries also became increasingly important. Today, work is undergoing yet another transformation as AI, automation, and machine learning are reshaping the economy and creating new opportunities and challenges for workers. Understanding the history of work can help us better navigate these changes and prepare for the future.

# TECHNOLOGICAL ADVANCEMENTS

Technology has been rapidly advancing in the past few decades. From the internet to smartphones, it has changed the way we work and communicate. The rise of technology has led to increased efficiency and productivity in the workplace. There are many ways in which technology has changed the way we work. One of the most significant technological advancements that has had a major impact on the workplace has been the development of computers. Computers have revolutionized the way we work. They have made it possible to store and access large amounts of data quickly and easily. This has made it easier for workers to do their jobs. For example, in the past, workers would have to manually sort through paper documents to find the information they needed. Today, they can simply search for it using a computer. Another major technological advancement that has impacted the workplace is the internet. The internet has made it possible for workers to communicate and share information across vast distances. This has made it easier for businesses to collaborate with partners and clients in other parts of the world. Finally, mobile technology has also had a significant impact on the way we work. Smartphones and tablets have made it possible for workers to stay connected to their work no matter where they are. This has made it easier for workers to stay productive while they are on the go. Overall, technological advancements have had a significant impact on the way we work. They have made it possible for workers to be more efficient and productive. As technology continues to advance, we can expect to see even more changes in the workplace.

## AUTOMATION AND ARTIFICIAL INTELLIGENCE

Automation and artificial intelligence (AI) are rapidly changing the nature of work. Automation refers to the use of technology to replace human labor, while AI involves the development of systems that can perform tasks requiring human intellect, like reasoning, learning, and decision-making. AI and automation have the potential to greatly improve efficiency and productivity in the workplace. However, it's important to recognize that these advances also have the potential to create job displacement and increase income inequality. It's crucial for individuals and organizations to understand the implications of automation and AI so that they can adapt to the changing landscape of work. This includes investing in education and training to develop the skills needed for the jobs of the future, embracing lifelong learning, and being comfortable with change. In the next chapter, we will explore the impact of automation on the workforce, including job losses and gains, skill requirements for new jobs, and the importance of education and training.

# Chapter 2: The Impact of Automation on the Workforce

Automation is rapidly changing the nature of the workforce and impacting jobs across various industries. In this chapter, we will explore the effects of automation on the workforce, job losses and gains, and skill requirements for new jobs.

## SUBCHAPTER 2.1: JOB LOSSES AND GAINS

As automation and AI continue to advance, many low-skilled jobs are at risk of being replaced by machines. However, it is important to note that automation also creates new job opportunities that require unique skill sets. For example, jobs related to software development, data analysis, and robotics are on the rise. It is crucial for individuals to stay informed about these job trends and adapt their skills accordingly.

# SUBCHAPTER 2.2: SKILL REQUIREMENTS FOR NEW JOBS

As new jobs emerge, the required skill sets are shifting from manual labor to technical and analytical skills. Employees who are adaptable and willing to learn new skills are more likely to thrive in this changing job market. In-demand skills include coding languages like Python and R, data analysis, machine learning, and cybersecurity.

# SUBCHAPTER 2.3: EDUCATION AND TRAINING

Education and training are crucial for workers to adapt to the changing nature of work. Formal education, such as college degrees and industry certifications, can provide valuable training and skills for new job opportunities. However, individuals can also take advantage of free online courses and resources to learn new skills and stay up-to-date with industry trends. Companies also have a responsibility to provide training and education opportunities to their employees to ensure that they remain relevant and competitive in the job market.

## SUBCHAPTER 2.1: JOB LOSSES AND GAINS

As technology continues to advance, there is no doubt that some jobs will become obsolete while others will emerge. There is no escaping the fact that automation will cause some job losses, particularly in industries such as manufacturing and logistics. However, it is important to note that automation will also create new jobs that require new skills. It is important to focus not just on the jobs that will be lost, but also the jobs that will be gained. According to the World Economic Forum, automation will create 2.1 million new jobs by 2025, particularly in fields such as data analysis, software development, and social media. While some workers may be worried about losing their jobs, it is important to look at the opportunities that automation will create. For example, automation will lead to increased productivity, which means that workers will be able to do more in less time, potentially leading to higher wages and more job security. Overall, it is important to have a balanced view of the effects of automation on the job market. While there will be job losses, it is important to remember that there will also be gains, particularly in fields related to technology and data. By staying informed and adaptable, workers can position themselves for success in the ever-changing job market.

## SKILL REQUIREMENTS FOR NEW JOBS

As automation and AI continue to disrupt traditional jobs, new roles are being created that require a different set of skills. The rise of technology has created a demand for workers with strong technical and digital skills. It's not just about being able to use basic software anymore, it's about being able to adapt to new technologies and use them to improve efficiency and productivity. One of the most crucial skills for the future job market is adaptability. As industries continue to change and evolve, workers need to be able to constantly learn and adapt to new systems and processes. This means being able to learn quickly and being open to trying new things. Another important skill is creativity. While AI may be able to perform certain tasks, it still lacks the ability to be truly creative and think outside the box. As a result, workers who are able to come up with innovative solutions and ideas will be highly valued in the future job market. Communication skills are also becoming increasingly important. As more companies embrace remote work and global teams, the ability to effectively communicate across different platforms and cultures is essential. Finally, in addition to technical skills, soft skills such as emotional intelligence and leadership are becoming more crucial. As AI takes on more repetitive tasks, it will be up to humans to provide the human touch in interpersonal interactions and leadership roles. Overall, the future job market will require workers with a diverse range of skills, both technical and soft. Those who are able to adapt and stay ahead of the curve will have a competitive edge in a constantly changing job market.

# EDUCATION AND TRAINING

As machines and automation become more prevalent in the workforce, it is becoming increasingly important to develop new skills and knowledge to stay competitive in the job market. Education and training are crucial components of adapting to the changing landscape of work. Traditional education routes, such as four-year degrees, may not always be necessary for certain jobs. In fact, some firms such as Google, Apple, and IBM no longer require a college degree for many of their positions. Instead, specialized training and vocational programs can be more efficient and cost-effective ways to prepare for new jobs. Employers may also be taking a larger role in employee education. They may offer job-specific training, mentorship programs, or tuition reimbursement for relevant courses or certifications. In addition, online education platforms such as Khan Academy, Udemy, and Coursera provide affordable and accessible ways to learn new skills and knowledge. It is important for individuals to regularly assess their skill set and continuously improve their knowledge to remain competitive in the job market. Whether through traditional education or on-the-job training programs, investing in education and training is essential for future success.

# Chapter 3: How to Stay Competitive in the Future Job Market

## SUBCHAPTER 3.1: RESKILLING AND UPSKILLING

In today's rapidly changing job market, reskilling and upskilling are essential for staying competitive. Reskilling involves learning new skills to transition to a new career or job field, while upskilling refers to developing new skills to enhance your current job performance. To stay ahead of the curve, it's important to continually assess your skills and identify areas where you can improve. There are many resources available for reskilling and upskilling, including online courses, training programs, and professional development opportunities. Take advantage of these resources to stay up-to-date with the latest industry trends and advancements.

# SUBCHAPTER 3.2: EMBRACING LIFELONG LEARNING

The concept of lifelong learning has become increasingly important in the modern job market. With technology advancing at such a fast pace, it's essential to continuously learn and adapt to new technologies and skills. Lifelong learning means committing to ongoing education and professional development, regardless of age or experience. There are many ways to embrace lifelong learning, such as taking online courses, attending workshops, joining professional organizations, and networking with peers in your industry. By dedicating yourself to learning, you can stay relevant and competitive in your field.

# SUBCHAPTER 3.3: NAVIGATING THE GIG ECONOMY

The gig economy refers to the increasing trend of temporary or freelance work, rather than traditional full-time employment. This trend has been driven by technology, which has made it easier for individuals to work independently and connect with clients all over the world. To succeed in the gig economy, it's important to develop a strong personal brand and network, as well as being highly adaptable and flexible. As a gig worker, you are essentially running your own business, which means taking charge of marketing, finances, and client management. In conclusion, staying competitive in the future job market requires a commitment to reskilling and upskilling, embracing lifelong learning, and navigating the gig economy. By staying on top of industry trends and continuously improving your skills, you can position yourself for success in the rapidly evolving world of work.

## RESKILLING AND UPSKILLING

The rapid advancement of technology and automation has led to the displacement of several jobs. As a result, it has become increasingly important for workers to reskill and upskill themselves to remain relevant in the job market. Reskilling refers to learning new skills that are different from the current job, while upskilling refers to upgrading existing skills to meet the demands of the current job market. One way to reskill is by networking with professionals in your desired field and participating in online learning programs. These could be MOOCs (Massive Open Online Courses), webinars, or online tutorials. You can also attend workshops or enroll in certification courses that are relevant to your desired field of work. Upskilling is essential to remain competitive in the workforce. To upskill yourself, you may want to identify skill gaps that are relevant to your job and focus on upgrading them. This may require taking courses, attending seminars, reading relevant books, or shadowing experienced colleagues. Companies also have a responsibility to offer training and development programs to their employees to ensure that they remain relevant and skilled in their area of work. Managers and supervisors should communicate the importance of upskilling and reskilling to their teams and encourage their employees to take an active role in their professional development. In summary, reskilling and upskilling are essential for workers to remain competitive in the job market. By continuously upgrading their skills, workers can ensure that they remain relevant and capable of adapting to new technological advancements. Moreover, companies that invest in the training and development of their employees can benefit from a more highly skilled workforce that is better equipped to serve their customers and remain competitive.

## EMBRACING LIFELONG LEARNING

In the age of AI, automation, and machine learning, it is no longer enough to simply obtain a degree or two and call it a day. The job landscape is changing rapidly, and it is important to constantly update your skillset in order to stay competitive. Embracing lifelong learning is not only necessary but also essential to remaining relevant in the job market. Fortunately, there are many ways to continue learning throughout your life. One way is to take online courses and webinars. There are numerous platforms such as Coursera, Udemy, and edX, which offer thousands of courses on a wide variety of subjects. These courses can be taken at your own pace and can often be completed for free or for a low cost. Another way to embrace lifelong learning is to attend workshops and conferences. These events are a great way to network with professionals in your field while also learning about the latest trends and technologies. They can be a bit pricey, but they are often worth the investment. Finally, reading industry publications and books can be a great way to stay up-to-date on the latest news and developments in your field. Make it a habit to read at least one book or article each week, and you will be amazed at how quickly your knowledge and understanding of your industry will grow. In conclusion, embracing lifelong learning is no longer an optional choice in the current job market. It is a necessary step towards staying competitive and relevant. By taking online courses, attending workshops and conferences, and reading industry publications, you can continue to grow and evolve alongside the job landscape.

## SUBCHAPTER 3.3: NAVIGATING THE GIG ECONOMY

The rise of the gig economy has revolutionized the way people work. Nowadays, more people than ever before are working on a freelance or contract basis, taking on short-term projects or gigs instead of traditional jobs. This kind of work offers a great deal of flexibility and can be very rewarding, but it also comes with its own set of challenges. One of the biggest challenges of the gig economy is finding and securing work. Unlike traditional jobs, where you have a steady salary and benefits, in the gig economy you are responsible for finding new projects and clients constantly. It can be difficult to build a reputation and network, but with the right approach, it is possible to create a sustainable career. Another challenge of the gig economy is managing your finances as a freelance or contract worker. You need to be aware of your tax obligations, and you should keep track of your expenses and income to make sure you are making enough money to support yourself. Fortunately, there are many resources available that can help you navigate the gig economy. Online platforms like Upwork and Fiverr can help you find new projects and clients, and networking events and professional associations can offer valuable support and advice. To succeed in the gig economy, it is important to develop a strong set of skills and a portfolio that showcases your work. You should also be willing to adapt and learn new skills as the market evolves. Overall, the gig economy offers an exciting and flexible way to work, but it does require a certain level of adaptability and self-reliance. With the right tools and strategy, however, you can thrive as a freelance or contract worker.

# Chapter 4: Preparing for the Rise of AI and Machine Learning

Artificial Intelligence (AI) and Machine Learning (ML) are rapidly becoming more prevalent in the modern workforce, and they are changing the landscape of jobs as we know it. In this chapter, we will explore the impact of AI and ML on the workplace and how to prepare for their rise.

# SUBCHAPTER 4.1: UNDERSTANDING AI AND MACHINE LEARNING

AI and ML are not new concepts, but they have recently gained traction in the realm of work. Simply put, AI refers to the capability of machines to perform tasks that would normally require human intelligence. ML, on the other hand, involves creating algorithms that enable computers to learn and improve upon tasks without being explicitly programmed. AI and ML have the potential to transform industries by making processes more efficient and reducing errors in decision-making. Some examples include chatbots that can handle customer inquiries and automated assistants that can schedule meetings and organize emails.

## Types of AI

There are two main types of AI: Narrow or Weak AI and General or Strong AI. Narrow AI is designed to perform a specific task, whereas General AI possesses human-like intelligence and is capable of adapting to various tasks. Currently, we only have Narrow AI available, but General AI is the subject of ongoing research.

## SUBCHAPTER 4.2: THE IMPACT OF AI ON THE WORKPLACE

AI has the potential to significantly impact the workforce, both positively and negatively. AI can automate tasks and increase productivity, but it can also lead to job losses as machines replace human labor. It is important to assess which jobs are at risk of being disrupted by AI and plan accordingly. However, it is important to note that AI can also create new jobs that require specific skill sets. The demand for jobs in data analysis and machine learning is increasing, and it is important to stay informed about these trends.

# AI and Ethics

As AI becomes more integrated into the workforce, it is important to consider the ethical implications. It is crucial to ensure that AI and ML algorithms are designed to be fair and unbiased. Companies must strive to mitigate the potential for AI to perpetuate existing inequalities.

## SUBCHAPTER 4.3: JOBS THAT WILL BE DISRUPTED BY AI

While AI and ML may lead to job losses in some industries, they may also create new job opportunities. Jobs with repetitive tasks such as data entry, assembly line work, and customer service may be at risk of being disrupted. However, jobs that require critical thinking, creativity, and emotional intelligence may see an increase in demand. It is important to stay informed about which industries may be affected by AI and plan accordingly. This may involve reskilling or upskilling to remain competitive in the evolving job market. Overall, it is important to embrace the potential of AI and ML while also preparing for their potential impact on the workforce.

## SUBCHAPTER 4.1: UNDERSTANDING AI AND MACHINE LEARNING

Artificial Intelligence (AI) and Machine Learning (ML) are transforming the way we work. AI is the ability of machines to mimic human cognition and undertake complex tasks that require human-like intelligence, while ML is a subset of AI that allows machines to learn and improve from data without being explicitly programmed. AI and ML are already being used to automate tasks like data entry, customer service, and routine administrative work. They are also being used to develop intelligent systems for decision-making, prediction, and analysis. In order to prepare for the future of work, it is important to have a basic understanding of AI and ML. This involves understanding the key technologies, concepts, and applications of these technologies in the workplace. Some of the key technologies used in AI and ML include Natural Language Processing (NLP), Computer Vision, and Deep Learning. These technologies are used to teach machines to recognize patterns, understand language, and analyze data in a way that is similar to human thinking. AI and ML have a broad range of potential applications in the workplace, including intelligent automation, predictive analytics, and virtual assistants. These technologies have the potential to improve productivity, reduce costs, and increase accuracy in a wide range of industries. However, there are also potential risks associated with these technologies, particularly in terms of job displacement and privacy concerns. It is important for workers to be aware of these potential risks and to develop strategies for adapting to a workplace that is increasingly driven by AI and ML. Overall, understanding AI and ML is essential for staying relevant in the future of work. By developing a basic understanding of these technologies, workers can position themselves for success in an increasingly automated and data-driven workplace.

## SUBCHAPTER 4.2: THE IMPACT OF AI ON THE WORKPLACE

Artificial Intelligence (AI) is no longer a thing of the future, but rather a tangible reality in today's workplace. Businesses are implementing AI technology to streamline operations and boost productivity. However, with this implementation, the workforce is also experiencing a significant impact. AI can perform a variety of tasks previously performed by humans. It can analyze complex data, recognize patterns and make critical decisions, among other things. As a result, some jobs that were once performed by humans are being replaced by machines. This shift means that current employees may need to learn new skills that complement and work alongside AI.

Additionally, employers may choose to hire individuals who have the necessary skills to work alongside AI systems. However, it is important to note that AI is not meant to completely replace the workforce, but rather to enhance it. AI technology is still limited in many ways, including emotional intelligence and the ability to think creatively. These are areas where humans excel and can therefore continue to play a vital role in the workforce. The rise of AI also means that there is a need for collaboration between humans and machines. Businesses need individuals who can work alongside AI and understand its capabilities to maximize its potential. As such, it is pivotal for employees to continuously upskill and stay up to date with technological advancements. As AI continues to transform the workforce, it is essential for businesses and employees to embrace the change and adapt accordingly. This means reskilling, training and hiring individuals with the right skills to work alongside AI systems. Those who can harness the power of AI and collaborate with machines are poised for career success in this new era of work. As technology continues to advance, more jobs are at risk of being replaced by AI and automation. While some jobs will simply be augmented by these technologies, others are likely to be completely disrupted. It is crucial to understand which industries and jobs are most at risk in order to prepare for the future of work. One sector that is particularly vulnerable to AI disruption is manufacturing. With the rise of robots and machines equipped with AI, many factory workers may find themselves out of work. In fact, a study by the McKinsey Global Institute found that up to 800 million workers worldwide could lose their jobs to automation by 2030, with manufacturing being one of the most affected industries. Another industry that is at risk is transportation, particularly jobs that involve driving. With the development of self-driving cars and trucks, there may be fewer opportunities for human drivers in the future. This could also have a ripple effect on related industries, such as shipping and logistics. Customer service jobs, particularly those that involve answering phones or responding to emails, are also at risk of being replaced by AI-powered chatbots and virtual assistants. Companies are already beginning to use these technologies to handle basic customer inquiries and support, and as the technology becomes more advanced, more jobs in this field are likely to be automated. Even highly skilled jobs, such as doctors and lawyers, are not immune to the potential disruption of AI and automation. AI is already being used to assist with medical diagnoses and legal research, and as these technologies continue to advance, they may begin to replace human workers in some tasks. It is important to note, however, that not all jobs are equally at risk of being disrupted by AI. Jobs that involve creativity, emotional intelligence, and critical thinking are less likely to be automated, as these are skills that are difficult for machines to replicate.

Overall, it is important to stay informed about the potential impact of AI on the job market, and to start thinking about how to prepare for the future of work. This may involve reskilling or upskilling in order to stay competitive in an ever-changing job market.

# Chapter 5: Embracing Change and Thriving in the Future

## SUBCHAPTER 5.1: ADAPTABILITY AND FLEXIBILITY

Being adaptable and flexible is crucial in today's rapidly changing work environment. The ability to quickly adjust to new situations and changes can set you apart from others in the job market. Employers are looking for individuals who are open to learning new skills and can adapt to new technologies. Adaptability is about being open to change and being willing to take on new challenges. It involves being able to learn and embrace new ideas and approaches. Flexibility means being able to adjust your work style and schedule to meet changing demands or priorities. It also means being open to working in different environments or with new teams. One way to improve your adaptability and flexibility is to seek out new experiences. Take on projects or tasks that are outside of your comfort zone. Attend training courses or workshops to learn new skills. Travel to new places and learn about different cultures. All of these experiences can help broaden your perspective and make you a more flexible and adaptable worker.

## SUBCHAPTER 5.2: INNOVATION AND ENTREPRENEURSHIP

Innovation and entrepreneurship are crucial skills for thriving in the future of work. These skills involve being able to identify new opportunities and create solutions to problems. In today's competitive job market, having an entrepreneurial mindset can set you apart from others and open up new career opportunities. Innovation involves thinking creatively and outside of the box. It requires being able to see opportunities where others see challenges. To become more innovative, start by observing the world around you. Look for inefficiencies or areas where improvement is needed. Brainstorm ideas and try to come up with new solutions to these problems. Entrepreneurship involves taking those innovative ideas and turning them into a business or career opportunity. This requires a combination of risk-taking, market analysis, and strategic planning. Even if you don't plan on starting your own business, having an entrepreneurial mindset can be valuable in any career path. It can help you identify new opportunities for growth and advancement.

# SUBCHAPTER 5.3: CREATING A CAREER DEVELOPMENT PLAN

Creating a career development plan is an important part of thriving in the future of work. This involves setting goals and identifying the steps you need to take to achieve them. It also involves regularly assessing your progress and making adjustments as needed. To create a career development plan, start by identifying your long-term career goals. Where do you see yourself in five or ten years? What skills or experiences do you need to acquire to get there? Once you have identified your goals, create a plan for achieving them. This may involve taking training courses, seeking out new experiences, or networking with people in your industry. It's important to regularly assess your progress and make adjustments to your plan as needed. This may involve changing your goals or adjusting the steps you need to take to achieve them. Regularly reassessing your plan can help ensure that you are staying on track and continuing to grow and develop in your career.

# ADAPTABILITY AND FLEXIBILITY

In today's fast-paced and constantly changing work environment, it is essential to remain adaptable and flexible in order to stay relevant and competitive. One of the key traits of successful individuals in the age of AI, automation, and machine learning is the ability to adapt to new situations and be open to change. Adaptability means being able to adjust to new circumstances and changing environments with ease. This includes being able to learn new skills quickly, being open to new ideas, and being able to think creatively to solve problems. Flexibility, on the other hand, refers to the ability to change plans or course of actions when necessary. Individuals who are adaptable and flexible are more likely to thrive in the future job market, as they can quickly adjust to the changes brought about by technological advancements. These traits are especially important for those in industries that are prone to disruption, such as manufacturing, transportation, and even healthcare. To become more adaptable and flexible, individuals can take a proactive approach towards learning new skills and expanding their knowledge base, as well as being open to new experiences and challenges.

## SUBCHAPTER 5.2: INNOVATION AND ENTREPRENEURSHIP

Innovation and entrepreneurship are essential skills for staying relevant in the future job market. Rather than just adapting to changes in the workplace, individuals with an entrepreneurial mindset actively seek out opportunities to create new solutions and add value to their organizations. To foster innovation, it is important to have a culture that encourages creativity and risk-taking. This could mean creating designated spaces for brainstorming, implementing idea-sharing platforms, or establishing regular innovation challenges. Entrepreneurship, on the other hand, involves taking an idea and turning it into a successful business venture. This requires a unique set of skills, including networking, marketing, financial management, and strategic planning. To become a successful entrepreneur, individuals must be willing to take calculated risks and persist through challenges. There are also opportunities to become an entrepreneur within an existing organization by starting a new department or launching a new product. This can involve pitching ideas to higher-ups, securing funding and resources, and building a team to bring the idea to fruition. Overall, having a mindset of innovation and entrepreneurship can not only help individuals stay relevant in the age of AI and automation but also lead to new and exciting career opportunities.

# CREATING A CAREER DEVELOPMENT PLAN

In today's fast-paced and dynamic job market, it's essential to have a career development plan. Having a well-thought-out plan can help you identify your strengths and weaknesses, make informed decisions, and stay on track to achieve your career goals. The first step in creating a career development plan is to determine your long-term career goals. Where do you see yourself in five or ten years? Once you have a clear vision of your ultimate career destination, you can start working backward to identify the skills and experiences you need to acquire to get there. It's essential to set achievable short-term goals that align with your long-term career goals. These goals should be specific, measurable, time-bound, and realistic. For instance, if you want to advance to a management position, a short-term goal could be taking a course or workshop to improve your leadership skills.

Networking is an essential part of career development. Building relationships with people in your industry or field can help you gain insights into trends and opportunities and give you access to potential mentors. Attend industry events, connect with others on professional social media platforms, and seek out opportunities to collaborate with colleagues on projects. In today's job market, it's crucial to stay up-to-date on industry trends and technological advances. Continuously developing your skillset and knowledge base will help you remain relevant and competitive. Take advantage of professional development opportunities, such as training programs, conferences, and workshops, to stay current on industry best practices. Remember, a career development plan is not set in stone. It's essential to regularly reassess your goals, adjust your plans, and pivot if necessary. Building a flexible mindset will help you adapt to new situations and unexpected challenges, which is critical for career success. Creating a career development plan may seem daunting, but it's an essential element in staying relevant in the age of AI, automation, and machine learning. By taking the time to identify your goals, develop your skills, build relationships, and stay current with industry trends, you can stay competitive and thrive in the ever-changing job market.

# Conclusion: The Future is Now

As we have seen throughout this book, the future of work is rapidly changing and it is happening right now. Jobs are being automated, artificial intelligence is becoming more prevalent, and the skills that are required to thrive in this new world are evolving. It is important to embrace this change and be adaptable and flexible. Those who are willing to reskill and upskill, embrace lifelong learning, and navigate the gig economy will be able to stay competitive in the future job market. Innovation and entrepreneurship will also be crucial in this new world. Those who are able to create and innovate will be able to take advantage of the new opportunities that arise. It is also important to create a career development plan for yourself. Take the time to reflect on your skills and interests, and identify where the new job opportunities are in your field. Consider what additional education or training you may need to stay relevant. In conclusion, the future of work is both exciting and daunting. However, with the right mindset and preparation, anyone can thrive in this new world. So, embrace the change, be proactive, and remember that the future is now.

## SUBCHAPTER 6.1: REFLECTIONS ON THE CHANGING NATURE OF WORK

As we come to the end of this book, it's important to take a moment to reflect on the changing nature of work. The last few decades have seen incredible technological advancements that have transformed the way we live and work. We've seen the rise of computers, the internet, and mobile devices, and now we're on the cusp of a new era of automation, artificial intelligence, and machine learning. As we've explored in this book, these changes will have a profound impact on the workforce. Some jobs will be lost to automation, while new jobs will be created that require different skills and abilities. It's clear that those who are able to adapt and embrace these changes will be best positioned for success in the future job market. But it's not just about adapting to new technologies. The nature of work itself is changing. We're seeing a rise in the gig economy, with more and more people choosing to work as freelancers or independent contractors. This has both benefits and drawbacks, but it's clear that traditional notions of work and employment are being challenged. Despite these changes, there are certain things that will always remain important in the world of work. Hard work, dedication, and a willingness to learn and grow will never go out of style. As we look to the future, it's important that we don't lose sight of what's truly important in our careers. In the end, the changing nature of work presents both challenges and opportunities. Those who are able to stay ahead of the curve and embrace change will be best positioned for success in the future. By approaching the future of work with an open mind and a willingness to learn, we can all thrive in the years ahead.

# FINAL THOUGHTS AND RECOMMENDATIONS

As we come to the end of this book, it is clear that the future of work is rapidly changing. The rise of automation, AI, and machine learning will continue to impact the workforce, and it is up to each individual to adapt and stay competitive in their chosen field. One of the most important things you can do is to continue learning and developing new skills throughout your career. Whether it is through formal education or on-the-job training, staying up-to-date with the latest technologies and best practices is essential for staying relevant in the job market. Another way to stay competitive is to embrace the gig economy, which offers flexible and varied work opportunities. This can be especially valuable for those who are looking to break into a new field or gain experience in multiple areas. Ultimately, it is important to remain adaptable and flexible in the face of change. Embracing new technologies and being willing to take risks can lead to exciting opportunities and career advancements. As you move forward in your career, remember to create a career development plan that outlines your goals and the steps you need to take to achieve them. And don't forget to continuously evaluate your progress and adjust your plan as necessary. The future is full of challenges and uncertainties, but with the right mindset and approach, you can thrive in the age of AI, automation, and machine learning.

Printed in Great Britain
by Amazon

31166581R00029